Solo and Duet Books

For the Piano

**Collected and Harmonized,
Edited and Fingered
by ANGELA DILLER
and ELIZABETH QUAILE**

FIRST SOLO BOOK
New Edition

→ SECOND SOLO BOOK
New Edition

THIRD SOLO BOOK

FOURTH SOLO BOOK

FIRST DUET BOOK

SECOND DUET BOOK

THIRD DUET BOOK

G. SCHIRMER, Inc.

DISTRIBUTED BY

HAL•LEONARD®
CORPORATION
7777 W. BLUEMOUND RD. P.O. BOX 13819 MILWAUKEE, WI 53213

ED. 3014

FOREWORD TO THE 1975 REVISED EDITION

In preparing this new edition of the Second Solo Book we have tried in every way to maintain the musical character and high standards of the work as Miss Diller and Miss Quaile envisaged it.

There are three main areas of change:

1. In order to make an easier transition from the First Solo Book to the Second, we have included a few less demanding pieces selected from the classic repertoire.

2. It is most important for students to learn early to observe the performance indications on the printed page. Therefore a glossary of musical terms has been added.

3. The editing of several pieces has been changed to conform to more recent research on performance practices in the Baroque and Classical periods.

We would like to express our thanks to Rose Simon for her editorial help and expert advice and to Mildred Bleier for her invaluable help in preparing the manuscript.

We hope this edition will continue to bring pleasure to new generations of piano students and will help to stimulate an interest in the world's great piano literature.

> Dorothy Weed
> Teacher at the Diller-Quaile School of Music
> 1922 to the present
> Music Director 1955-1972
>
> Robert Fraley
> Teacher at the Diller-Quaile School of Music
> 1961 to the present
> Director since 1972

INDEX OF TITLES

Second Solo Book

St. Paul's Steeple

English

I Saw Three Ships

Allegretto

English

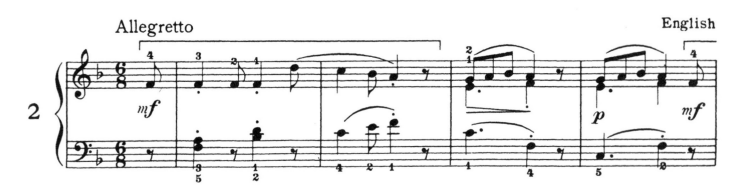

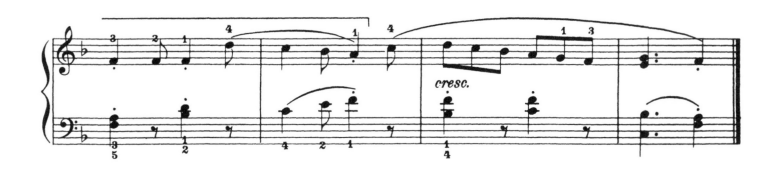

Sleep, Baby, Sleep

Andante

German

The Shepherdess

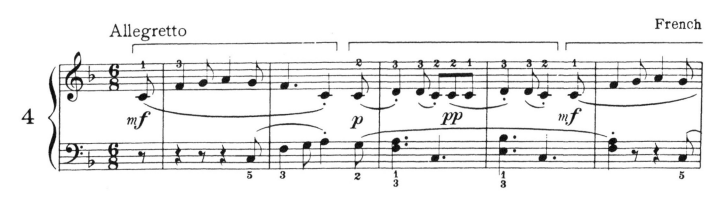

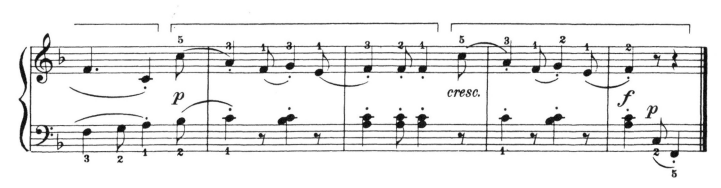

Christmas Song

4

The Tiny Man

Dutch

Cradle-Song

French

Two Russian Folk-Tunes

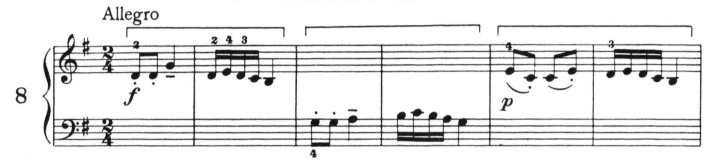

Willy, Willy, Will

Allegro

German

9

French Song

Allegretto

10

German Folk-Tune

In Holland Stands a House

Dutch

Flemish Song

Swabian Folk-Dance

Da Capo

Melody in A Minor

Russian

Happy New Year

French

Allegretto

Joseph Haydn
(1732 - 1809)

Bourrée

Leopold Mozart
(1719 - 1787)

Song of the Boatman

Andante con moto

Russian

19

Bergerette

Moderato

French

20

Song of the Shepherdess

French

Écossaise

Ludwig van Beethoven
(1770 - 1827)

Old French Drinking-Song

Minuet in F major

Wolfgang Amadeus Mozart
(1756-1791)

Gavotte and Musette

Old French

Old French Air

Minuet Provençal

French Melody

Allegretto un poco moderato

Minuet in G major

W. A. Mozart

Two French Folk-Tunes

Soldiers' March

Robert Schumann
(1810-1856)

Allegro deciso

Allegro

W.A.Mozart

31

Two Minuets

I

Allegretto

J.S.Bach

32

Fine

II

D.C. Menuet I al Fine

Bon Voyage, M. Dumolet!

French Folk-Tune

Musette

Johann Sebastian Bach
(1685-1750)

Sonatina

L. van Beethoven

V. S.

Romanza
Allegretto

Shepherd Playing on His Pipe

Vladimir I. Rebikov
(1866-1920)

GLOSSARY

Signs

Legato. Smoothly, well connected, flowing. (Italian)

Staccato. Detached, separated. Play with an up-stroke rather than a down stroke. (Italian)

Portato. Between staccato and legato. Usually more legato than staccato. (Italian)

Tenuto. Hold the note for its full value. (Italian)

Forte Tenuto. Somewhat staccato. Emphasize each note separately.

Fermata. Hold the note longer than its written value. (Italian)

Crescendo. Growing louder and louder. (Italian)

Diminuendo. Growing softer and softer. (Italian)

Accent mark. The note is suddenly played louder.

Tie. Play the first note and hold it for the combined value of both notes. Do not play the second note — listen to it.

Slur. A curved line meaning to connect smoothly the notes under it or above it.

Phrase marks. Indicating a long or short musical idea or phrase. Usually the curved line means to play legato as well.

A comma. Indicating a break in the phrase.

Repeat sign. Go back to the beginning and play the passage again.

With this sign, repeat only the music between the dots.

Tempo Words

(Italian words that indicate the tempo)

Allegro	Fast.	*Andantino*	Not quite as slow as *Andante*
Allegretto	Lively but not as fast as *Allegro*.	*Moderato*	At a moderate, slow tempo.
Andante	Slow but moving. (Literally, "walking.")		

Dynamics

(Italian words that tell you how loud or soft the music should sound.)

ff	*fortissimo*	Very loud.	**p**	*piano*	Soft.
f	*forte*	Loud.	**pp**	*pianissimo*	Very soft.
mf	*mezzo forte*	Medium loud. (*Mezzo* means half.)	**sf**	*sforzando*	A sudden accent on a single chord or note. Not to be confused with **f** which refers to the whole passage.
mp	*mezzo piano*	Medium soft.			

Pianoforte — The full name of the piano. It was invented in 1709 by an Italian, Bartolommeo Christofori, and was so called because it was the first keyboard instrument that could play both soft and loud.

General Musical Terms

Accomp. pp	Play the accompaniment very softly.	*Cresc.*	Abbreviation for *crescendo*. Growing louder and louder. (Italian)
Air	A tune or melody.	*Da capo*	Go back to the beginning and play to *fine* which is the finish or end. Omit any repeats in the *da capo*. (Italian)
Cantabile	Like a song. Make the melody sing. (Italian)	*Da capo al fine*	
Con brio	With fire and excitement. (Italian)	*Deciso*	Energetic; decided. (Italian)
Con moto	With motion; moving; animated. (Italian)	*Dim.*	Abbreviation for *diminuendo*. Growing softer and softer. (Italian)

General Music Terms
(continued)

Fermata	A pause. Hold the note longer than its written value. (Italian)
Fine	The end. (Italian)
Gavotte	A dance of French origin with a lively rhythm in ₵ $\left(\frac{2}{2}\text{ meter}\right)$ counted 2 | 1 or in C $\left(\frac{4}{4}\text{ meter}\right)$ counted 3 4 | 1 2.
Gioioso	Joyfully; gaily; merrily. (Italian)
Grazioso	Gracefully. (Italian)
l.h.	Left hand.
Minuet	A slow, elegant, stately dance from France in $\frac{3}{4}$ meter, counted either | 1 2 3 or 3 | 1 2.
Musette	1. An old instrument like a small bagpipe with a drone bass.
	2. A piece in the rhythm of a gavotte which is called a musette because it has a drone bass. (See No. 30.) The Bach *Musette*, (No. 32) seems to be an exception since it is written in $\frac{2}{4}$ meter. However, If you put two measures together and count 3 4 | 1 2 you will find it has the feeling of Musette rhythm. The repeated octaves in the left hand give somewhat the effect of a drone bass.

Poco	A little. (Italian)
Rall.	Abbreviation for *rallentando*. Growing slower and slower. (Italian)
Rit. Ritard.	Abbreviation for *ritardando*. Same as rall. (Italian)
r.h.	Right hand.
Romanza	A melodious piece. (Italian)
Semplice	Simply. (Italian)
Sempre	Always; throughout. (Italian)
Simile	Continue in the same way. (Italian)
Sonatina	A little sonata. (A sonata is a long, difficult piece in several contrasting parts called movements.) (Italian)
Swabian Folk Dance	A peasant dance from Swabia, a mountainous region in southwest Germany.
Tenuto	Hold the note for its full value. (Italian)
Tie	A curved line connecting two notes. Play the first note and hold it for the value of both notes combined. Do not play the second note. Listen to it.
Trio	The middle part of a minuet.
V.S. Volti subito	Turn the page quickly. (Italian)